Francis Frith's
ESSEX
LIVING MEMORIES

photographs of the mid twentieth century

Francis Frith's

ESSEX
LIVING MEMORIES

Frances Clamp

FRITH
BOOK Co

First published in the United Kingdom in 2002 by
Frith Book Company Ltd

Hardback Edition 2002
ISBN 1-85937-490-5

British Library Cataloguing in Publication Data

Francis Frith's Essex Living Memories
Frances Clamp

Frith Book Company Ltd
Frith's Barn, Teffont,
Salisbury, Wiltshire SP3 5QP
Tel: +44 (0) 1722 716 376
Email: info@francisfrith.co.uk
www.francisfrith.co.uk

Printed and bound in Great Britain

Front Cover: Southend-on-Sea, The Boating Lake c1950 S155020

contents

Francis Frith : Victorian Pioneer

FRANCIS FRITH, Victorian founder of the world-famous photographic archive, was a complex and multi-talented man. A devout Quaker and a highly successful Victorian businessman, he was both philosophic by nature and pioneering in outlook.

By 1855 Francis Frith had already established a wholesale grocery business in Liverpool, and sold it for the astonishing sum of £200,000, which is the equivalent today of over £15,000,000. Now a multi-millionaire, he was able to indulge his passion for travel. As a child he had pored over travel books written by early explorers, and his fancy and imagination had been stirred by family holidays to the sublime mountain regions of Wales and Scotland. 'What a land of spirit-stirring and enriching scenes and places!' he had written. He was to return to these scenes of grandeur in later years to 'recapture the thousands of vivid and tender memories', but with a different purpose. Now in his thirties, and captivated by the new science of photography, Frith set out on a series of pioneering journeys to the Nile regions that occupied him from 1856 until 1860.

Intrigue and Adventure

He took with him on his travels a specially-designed wicker carriage that acted as both dark-room and sleeping chamber. These far-flung journeys were packed with intrigue and adventure. In his life story, written when he was sixty-three, Frith tells of being held captive by bandits, and of fighting 'an awful midnight battle to the very point of surrender with a deadly pack of hungry, wild dogs'. Sporting flowing Arab costume, Frith arrived at Akaba by camel seventy years before Lawrence, where he encountered 'desert princes and rival sheikhs, blazing with jewel-hilted swords'.

During these extraordinary adventures he was assiduously exploring the desert regions bordering the Nile and patiently recording the antiquities and peoples with his camera. He was the first photographer to venture beyond the sixth cataract. Africa was still the mysterious 'Dark Continent', and Stanley and Livingstone's historic meeting was a decade into the future. The conditions for picture taking confound belief. He laboured for hours in his wicker dark-room in the sweltering heat of the desert, while the volatile chemicals fizzed dangerously in their trays. Often he was forced to work in remote tombs and caves where conditions were cooler. Back in London he exhibited his photographs and was 'rapturously cheered' by members of the Royal Society. His reputation as a photographer was made overnight. An eminent modern historian has likened their impact on the population of the time to that on our own generation of the first photographs taken on the surface of the moon.

Venture of a Life-Time

Characteristically, Frith quickly spotted the opportunity to create a new business as a specialist publisher of photographs. He lived in an era of immense and sometimes violent change. For the poor in the early part of Victoria's reign work was a drudge and the hours long, and people had precious little free time to enjoy themselves. Most had no transport other than a cart or gig at their disposal, and had not travelled far beyond the boundaries of their own town or village. However,

by the 1870s, the railways had threaded their way across the country, and Bank Holidays and half-day Saturdays had been made obligatory by Act of Parliament. All of a sudden the ordinary working man and his family were able to enjoy days out and see a little more of the world.

With characteristic business acumen, Francis Frith foresaw that these new tourists would enjoy having souvenirs to commemorate their days out. In 1860 he married Mary Ann Rosling and set out with the intention of photographing every city, town and village in Britain. For the next thirty years he travelled the country by train and by pony and trap, producing fine photographs of seaside resorts and beauty spots that were keenly bought by millions of Victorians. These prints were painstakingly pasted into family albums and pored over during the dark nights of winter, rekindling precious memories of summer excursions.

The Rise of Frith & Co

Frith's studio was soon supplying retail shops all over the country. To meet the demand he gathered about him a small team of photographers, and published the work of independent artist-photographers of the calibre of Roger Fenton and Francis Bedford. In order to gain some understanding of the scale of Frith's business one only has to look at the catalogue issued by Frith & Co in 1886: it runs to some 670 pages, listing not only many thousands of views of the British Isles but also many photographs of most European countries, and China, Japan, the USA and Canada – note the sample page shown above from the hand-written *Frith & Co* ledgers detailing pictures taken. By 1890 Frith had created the greatest specialist photographic publishing company in the

world, with over 2,000 outlets – more than the combined number that Boots and W H Smith have today! The picture on the right shows the *Frith & Co* display board at Ingleton in the Yorkshire Dales. Beautifully constructed with mahogany frame and gilt inserts, it could display up to a dozen local scenes.

Postcard Bonanza

The ever-popular holiday postcard we know today took many years to develop. In 1870 the Post Office issued the first plain cards, with a pre-printed stamp on one face. In 1894 they allowed other publishers' cards to be sent through the mail with an attached adhesive halfpenny stamp. Demand grew rapidly, and in 1895 a new size of postcard was permitted called the court card, but there was little room for illustration. In 1899, a

year after Frith's death, a new card measuring 5.5 x 3.5 inches became the standard format, but it was not until 1902 that the divided back came into being, with address and message on one face and a full-size illustration on the other. *Frith & Co* were in the vanguard of postcard development, and Frith's sons Eustace and Cyril continued their father's monumental task, expanding the number of views offered to the public and recording more and more places in Britain, as the coasts and countryside were opened up to mass travel.

Francis Frith died in 1898 at his villa in Cannes, his great project still growing. The archive he created continued in business for another seventy years. By 1970 it contained over a third of a million pictures of 7,000 cities, towns and villages. The massive photographic record Frith has left to us stands as a living monument to a special and very remarkable man.

Frith's Archive: A Unique Legacy

FRANCIS FRITH'S legacy to us today is of immense significance and value, for the magnificent archive of evocative photographs he created provides a unique record of change in 7,000 cities, towns and villages throughout Britain over a century and more. Frith and his fellow studio photographers revisited locations many times down the years to update their views, compiling for us an enthralling and colourful pageant of British life and character.

We tend to think of Frith's sepia views of Britain as nostalgic, for most of us use them to conjure up memories of places in our own lives with which we have family associations. It often makes us forget that to Francis Frith they were records of daily life as it was actually being lived in the cities, towns and villages of his day. The Victorian age was one of great and often bewildering change for ordinary people, and though the pictures evoke an impression of slower times, life was as busy and hectic as it is today.

We are fortunate that Frith was a photographer of the people, dedicated to recording the minutiae of everyday life. For it is this sheer wealth of visual data, the painstaking chronicle of changes in dress, transport, street layouts, buildings, housing, engineering and landscape that captivates us so much today. His remarkable images offer us a powerful link with the past and with the lives of our ancestors.

Today's Technology

Computers have now made it possible for Frith's many thousands of images to be accessed almost instantly. In the Frith archive today, each photograph is carefully 'digitised' then stored on a CD Rom. Frith archivists can locate a single photograph amongst thousands within seconds. Views can be catalogued and sorted under a variety of categories of place and content to the immediate benefit of researchers.

Inexpensive reference prints can be created for them at the touch of a mouse button, and a wide range of books and other printed materials assembled and published for a wider, more general readership - in the next twelve months over a hundred Frith local history titles will be published! The day-to-day workings of the archive are very different from how they were in Francis Frith's time: imagine the herculean task of sorting through eleven tons of glass negatives as Frith had to do to locate a particular sequence of pictures!

THE FRANCIS FRITH COLLECTION

Photographic publishers since 1860

HOME | PHOTO SEARCH | BOOKS | PORTFOLIO | GALLERY | MY CART
Products | History | Other Collections | Contact us | Help?

your town,
your village

365,000 photographs of 7,000 towns and villages, taken between 1860 & 1970.

The Frith Archive
The Frith Archive is the remarkable legacy of its energetic and visionary founder. Today, the Frith archive is the only nationally important archive of its kind still in private ownership.

The Collection is world-renowned for the extraordinary quality of its images.

The Gallery
This month The Frith Gallery features images from "Frith's Egypt".

News...
Image update complete.
An additional 5,000 images have been added and the quality of all images has now been improved.

Sample Chapters avaliable.
The first selection of sample chapters from the Frith Book Co.'s extensive range is now available. All are offered in Pdf format for easy downloading and viewing.

explore FRITH
Search thousands of photographs from one of the worlds' great archives.

Town search

GO

County search
Select a county

GO

the FRITHgallery

See Frith at www.francisfrith.co.uk

Yet the archive still prides itself on maintaining the same high standards of excellence laid down by Francis Frith, including the painstaking cataloguing and indexing of every view.

It is curious to reflect on how the internet now allows researchers in America and elsewhere greater instant access to the archive than Frith himself ever enjoyed. Many thousands of individual views can be called up on screen within seconds on one of the Frith internet sites, enabling people living continents away to revisit the streets of their ancestral home town, or view places in Britain where they have enjoyed holidays. Many overseas researchers welcome the chance to view special theme selections, such as transport, sports, costume and ancient monuments.

We are certain that Francis Frith would have heartily approved of these modern developments in imaging techniques, for he himself was always working at the very limits of Victorian photographic technology.

The Value of the Archive Today

Because of the benefits brought by the computer, Frith's images are increasingly studied by social historians, by researchers into genealogy and ancestory, by architects, town planners, and by teachers and schoolchildren involved in local history projects.

In addition, the archive offers every one of us an opportunity to examine the places where we and our families have lived and worked down the years. Highly successful in Frith's own era, the archive is now, a century and more on, entering a new phase of popularity.

Historians consider the Francis Frith Collection to be of prime national importance. It is the only archive of its kind remaining in private ownership and has been valued at a million pounds. However, this figure is now rapidly increasing as digital technology enables more and more people around the world to enjoy its benefits.

Francis Frith's archive is now housed in an historic timber barn in the beautiful village of Teffont in Wiltshire. Its founder would not recognize the archive office as it is today. In place of the many thousands of dusty boxes containing glass plate negatives and an all-pervading odour of photographic chemicals, there are now ranks of computer screens. He would be amazed to watch his images travelling round the world at unimaginable speeds through network and internet lines.

The archive's future is both bright and exciting. Francis Frith, with his unshakeable belief in making photographs available to the greatest number of people, would undoubtedly approve of what is being done today with his lifetime's work. His photographs, depicting our shared past, are now bringing pleasure and enlightenment to millions around the world a century and more after his death.

Essex - An Introduction

ESSEX MUST BE one of the most misunderstood counties in the country. The image often presented is of a flat, rather dull place. This is completely undeserved. Essex is steeped in history. It has beautiful towns and villages, and some of the most notable churches to be found anywhere in England.

In the south-west of the county London is close by, yet even here the countryside encroaches and each town has its own individuality. To the north-west many of the villages are almost untouched by the march of time. On the southern border, beside the River Thames, are the busy towns of Purfleet, Grays and the port of Tilbury. To the east lie the brooding ruins of Hadleigh Castle and the old fishing village of Leigh-on-Sea. Yet further along the coast comes the bustling brightness of Southend, with its famous pier stretching out into the estuary. Each of these towns shows a different face of Essex.

Along the east coast, creeks and marshes have their own wild beauty. Northwards comes another major seaside town, Clacton. Here it is possible to recall the summer days of childhood spent on golden beaches, with ice creams and candy floss always available nearby. Yet further north lies the port of Harwich, now a gateway to the continent.

Moving into the centre of the county, we come to the large, busy towns of Colchester and Chelmsford, both steeped in their own unique history. Chelmsford is the administrative centre of the county, and has had its own cathedral since 1913. Colchester was of great importance during the time of the Roman occupation of Britain. The town is still dominated by an important garrison. Then, too, there are the new

towns of Basildon and Harlow with their carefully planned residential areas, shopping centres and numerous amenities.

The county covers 3,670 square kilometres (1,417 square miles). It is roughly square in shape, with its boundaries mainly defined by water - the River Stour to the north, the rivers Stort and Lea (or Lee) to the west, the mighty Thames to the south and the North Sea to the east.

Because Colchester was of such importance to the Romans, a good communications system was necessary, and a long straight road was built to link the town with London. Although the A12 has been widened and altered, it follows much of the old route. Today part of the M25 can be found in the south-west, with the M11 heading northwards. But twisting lanes that have survived the centuries remain; new surfaces now cover many of the old dirt tracks, and some of the bends have been removed, but the routes they follow and the fields they pass are little changed.

Apart from one or two outcrops of chalk, Essex is largely a county of clay, both London clay and boulder clay. Sand and gravel have also been widely quarried. The lack of natural rock meant that stone for important buildings had to be imported - a costly matter. No wonder local craftsmen became skilled in the use of wood and in brick-making. These are the materials used in many of the traditional Essex houses. One of the chalk outcrops occurs at Purfleet, and has been used for the production of cement. The towering chimneys here are well-known landmarks to those travelling on the M25.

Those who have visited Essex only fleetingly may describe the county as flat and uninteresting, but this is very far from the truth. There are gentle hills, notably at Laindon and Danbury, and horses drawing carriages from London up Brook Street into Brentwood in bygone days would hardly have thought of Essex as flat!

Essex soil lends itself to farming. Ideal for the growing of corn, the land has also been used for market gardening, and in recent years many fields have turned bright yellow in the spring with oilseed rape. There is also some dairy and mixed farming. A number of the photographs in this book show the farms and villages of the county. Where corn grows, there is also the need for mills; many picturesque windmills and water mills from the past can still be seen. Fine examples of surviving windmills include those at Stansted Mountfitchet, Thaxted and Tiptree.

From earliest times there was settlement in Essex. More than 150 traces of Stone Age settlements have been recorded. Later, with the coming of the Romans, a fine temple was built at Colchester. This was destroyed during the

British rebellion against Roman rule, led by Boudicca, Queen of the Iceni. Colchester Castle now stands on the site.

The county's name dates from the time when the Saxons invaded the east of the country; for a while, in the 7th century, it became a kingdom. It was in this century too that St Cedd reintroduced Christianity to this part of Britain. His church of St Peter-on-the-Wall at Bradwell was built on the site of the gatehouse of a former Roman fort, and distinctive Roman bricks can be seen in the walls. At one time it served as his cathedral. This ancient chapel stands on a desolate part of the coast, at the end of an uneven track that has been trodden by thousands over the centuries. It is now a centre of pilgrimage, and is believed to be the oldest surviving church in England. In complete contrast, within two miles of the church and close to the estuary of the River Blackwater stands a 20th-century nuclear power station.

There are many beautiful churches in the county, both large and small. The church of St Andrew at Greensted-juxta-Ongar has walls made of vertical oak tree trunks, split and with the flat side facing inwards. Originally these were set into a massive beam, but in the mid 19th century this beam was replaced with brick supports. The timbers are original, and some have been dated to 850 AD, thus making this the oldest wooden church in England surviving

from Saxon times. One of the grandest churches in the county must be the church of St John the Baptist, St Mary and St Lawrence in Thaxted - St Lawrence is the patron saint of cutlers, a craft for which the town was renowned. The spire soars above the houses, reaching to a height of 181ft.

In a county with the boundaries marked out by water, it is hardly surprising that rivers and the sea have played an important part in its development. The marshy coast with its creeks and inlets lent itself to fishing and at times to smuggling. Many stories are told of the contraband brought in and hidden away in taverns and other convenient buildings close to the shore.

Essex is rich in ancient taverns, and many newer ones too. It is almost impossible to find a village without at least one inn, and many have far more. As for the towns, the traveller is often spoilt for choice.

The shopping centres at Basildon and Harlow have already been mentioned. However, in recent years the Lakeside Shopping Centre has been developed. In the shadow of the Queen Elizabeth II Bridge, the longest cable-stayed bridge in Europe, and close to the Dartford tunnels, this massive complex is visited each year by around 24 million people.

An airfield at Stansted was used during the Second World War. In 1967 it was decided that Stansted should become the third London

airport, although this caused much local outcry. Southend too has its own airport, and a number of other sites around the county were used as air bases during the two wars of the 20th century. One of these was at North Weald, and close by is the King's Head, featured in this book. Southend now has an impressive annual air display.

No account of the county would be complete without mention of the great Forest of Essex. This was a royal forest. Over the years its size has diminished, but there are still large areas of woodland at Epping and Hatfield Broad Oak. In the Middle Ages Epping Forest was known as Waltham Forest, and a third of the remaining forest land lies within the parish of Waltham Abbey.

Other green areas have become of great importance in recent years, including a green belt intended to curtail further London spread. A number of country parks are to be found in the county, including the beautiful South Weald and Thorndon Parks close to Brentwood. On the west side of Chelmsford there is Highlands Park; the Lee Valley Regional Park has its main information centre at Waltham Abbey; and there is a large area of open land around Hadleigh Castle, overlooking the River Thames. As well as these and other large green spaces, each town has at least one park and many are of outstanding beauty.

In the following pages we will find many reminders of Essex from half a century ago. Some places have changed almost beyond recognition, yet the camera has frozen them in time so that old memories may be renewed. In other places little has altered, at least on the surface; but traffic has increased, the old names of stores, once well known in every household, have long since passed into history, and clothing styles have inevitably changed. Essex is a beautiful county, well worth taking the time to explore in depth.

The North-West

Stansted Mountfitchet
Lower Street c1965 S281014
This attractive town was the site of a timber castle belonging to
the Montfitchet family, from whom it takes its name. The castle
was destroyed in the time of King John, but has now been
reconstructed. In the foreground of the photograph we can see a
beautiful and well-preserved timber-framed house, known as
Savages. Facing us is the Kings Arms hotel, with the Queens Head
the first white building on the right.

Stansted Mountfitchet, The Mill c1965 S281023
Built in 1787, this fine tower mill is listed as an Ancient Monument. It is in an excellent state of preservation, and the public has limited access. Close by is St Theresa's Catholic church.

▼ Newport, The Tolls c1960 N27027

The Toll House stands beside a bridge over the River Cam. Here farmers were once required to pay for the right to take their livestock across this bridge. At least the people of Newport were apparently exempt from the payment of tolls.

▼ Newport, Church Street Cottages c1960 N27036

These unusual cottages are half thatched and half tiled. At one time striped sunblinds of the type protecting the third door were very popular. Nearby is the church of St Mary the Virgin, parts of which date from the 14th century.

▲ Saffron Walden High Street c1950

S43012

The town boasts a maze that goes back to prehistoric times. Most of the buildings we see here remain much the same, although their functions have altered. Single-decker buses wait on opposite sides of the road. Note the straight-backed cars, many still with running boards. The church is dedicated to St Mary the Virgin.

◄ **Saffron Walden
Fry's Garden c1950**
S43008
This small garden is to be found in Bridge End Gardens. The photograph was taken from a viewing platform and, bathed in sunlight, the neatly trimmed hedges are impressive. Unfortunately, most of the bushes, although still cared for, have now lost their distinctive shapes. The fountain in the middle of the pond has now gone.

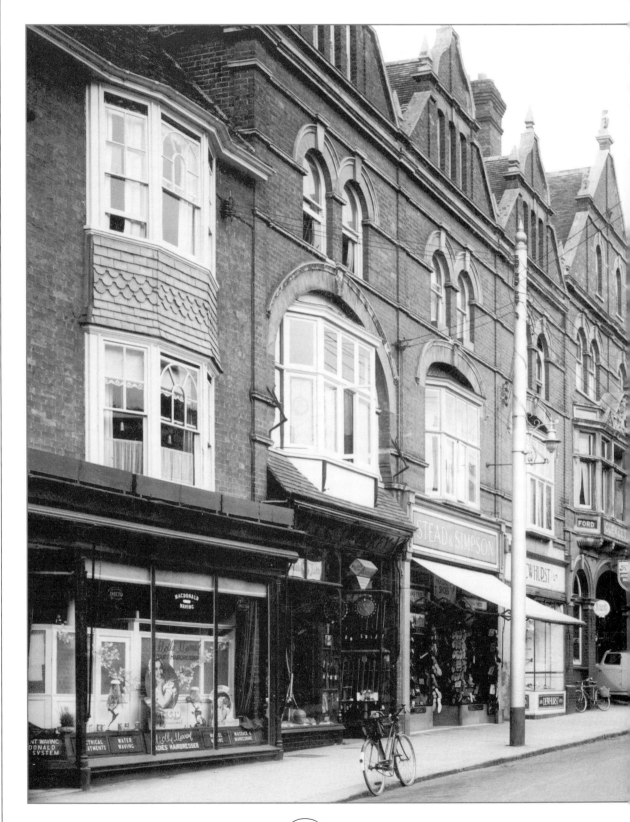

**Saffron Walden
King Street c1950**
S43001
The saffron crocus,
once very important in
the dyeing industry,
gave the town its name.
Many of these
substantial buildings
remain; however, the
garage has gone, and
the building has been
taken over by W H
Smith. The Hoops is no
longer an inn, and the
premises are now used
as a shop.

◀ **Wimbush, The Village Shop c1950** W197007 Here we see a typical scene to be found in rural Essex. The bungalow on the left serves as a shop, and the vehicle outside belonged to Fred Derby & Sons. Close by, almost hidden by the trees, are pleasant cottages.

Saffron Walden, Market Place c1950 S43035

The fine old building on the right is used as the Town Hall. A blue plaque commemorates the fact that John Newman was burnt at the stake for his Protestant faith in August 1555. Designed by John Bentley, the drinking fountain on the left was exhibited at the Imperial Exhibition of 1862 and presented to the town to commemorate the marriage of the Prince of Wales, later to be Edward VII.

▼ Wimbush, Aldridge's Cottage c1960 W197018

The ancient art of the thatcher has been caught in this interesting photograph. Many Essex villages have fine examples of thatched buildings. This weather-board cottage has now been considerably altered, although many of the features we see here are still apparent.

◄ Great Sampford High Street c1955

G91009

This narrow road hardly looks like a high street! On the side of the house facing us is the date 1595. Behind the trees on the left is the church of St Michael. Note the fine example of thatching on the buildings in the foreground.

Thaxted, Old Almshouses c1955 T28016
These beautiful almshouses stand close to the magnificent Thaxted church. In the background we can see John Webb's Mill - it was named after the owner of the land on which it was built. It dates from 1804, but was derelict by the 1950s. The mill has been restored, and in 1991 the sails were re-erected.

Thaxted, The Guildhall c1955 T28045
This fine timber-framed guildhall dates from the late 15th century. It was built by the powerful cutlers, who were active in the town in the 14th and 15th centuries. The magnificent church of St John the Baptist, St Mary and St Lawrence has a 181ft spire.

Elsenham, Elsenham Hall c1965 E231010
Sir Walter Gilbey, whose name is associated with the Elsenham Jam Company, at one time lived at Elsenham Hall, a house set in wooded parkland. A picture of the magnificent house appeared on the jam jar labels.

Great Easton, The Village c1955 G95009
This is a typical quiet Essex village, with some impressive timber-framed houses. The cross in the centre of the picture is a memorial to those killed in both the First and Second World Wars. The Bell Stores, shown on the right, is now a private house.

▼ **Dunmow, The Tudor Town Hall c1965** D90062

The building on the left is the Tudor Town Hall, also known as the Town House or Geld Hall. It was certainly in existence in 1571, and is now occupied by Trembath Welch, the estate agents. J M Welch & Son moved into the Town Hall in 1886, paying an annual rent of £10. By the early 1930s the building had deteriorated, and in 1935 Mr C J M Welsh bought it for £600 and set about careful restoration to bring it back as near as possible to its original condition. The results are impressive.

▼ **Felsted, The Village c1960** F76007

Felsted is well known for its fine public school. In this photograph, we see the original school building, known as the Old School House, facing the camera. The school was founded in 1564 by Richard, Lord Riche, Lord Chancellor for two years in the reign of Edward VI. To the right of the picture stands Bootes House Café - an interesting inscription reads 'George Boote Made This House 1596'.

▲ **Stebbing, High Street c1960** S282014

This scene has changed little in the years since the photograph was taken. Many of the houses have attractive pargeting, including Butlers Cottage on the right of the picture. The leaning timber-framed house on the left is known as Tudor Cottage.

◄ Rayne, Old Cottages and the Church c1960 R12004
The old house on the right has now been restored, but the seat on which the man rests is no more. Apart from these changes, this scene is little altered. All Saints' church, seen in the background, has a west tower of red brick dating from Tudor times. Sir William Capel, a Lord Mayor of London, had this erected in 1510.

Braintree, The Fountain c1955 B178001
William Julian Courtauld, of Pennypot in Halstead, gave this fountain to the town of Braintree in memory of King George V. The church of St Michael underwent alterations in Victorian times, but the tower with its shingled spire dates from the 13th century.

Braintree, Bocking End c1955 B178032

Bocking and Braintree now merge into one. Here we see busy shoppers, but little traffic - one man (centre right) is even able to pause in the middle of the road to pick something up! The White Hart has changed little over the years, but the imposing clock tower, and the shops to its right, have now been replaced by a large modern store.

Bocking, Bradford Street c1950 B126011

These old buildings in this quiet street remain virtually unchanged. Many on the left have traces of pargeting. Note the large chimney pots, dating back to a time when open fires were the only form of heating.

Bocking
Bradford Street c1950
B126012
Here we see the same road as the one shown in B126011, but from the opposite direction. In most cases, doors open straight onto the street. Little traffic can be seen.

◄ **Finchingfield
The Village c1960**
F77048
This much-photographed picture-book village rises above a green and a pond, which is fed by a stream - a tributary of the River Pant. On the right is the war memorial. The village is now a popular coach halt in summer, and there are many cafés and souvenir shops. The church of St John the Baptist dominates the scene.

Wethersfield
The Village c1965
W192012

This quiet scene was taken from across the small village green. In the foreground, on the left, is the village hall. Next door stands the Co-operative Society store, with cycles left on the ground outside - this shop has now become a restaurant. Close by is the church of St Mary and St Mary Magdalene.

Toppesfield
The Village Pump
c1960   T119001

The imposing pump stands at a cross roads in the village. An inscription warns all users to first boil any water taken for drinking purposes - the possible consequences of ignoring this advice are not given. Behind the pump we can see a tractor and trailer.

Great Yeldham
The Old Oak c1960
G324013

The sad remains of this once great tree have suffered further since this photograph was taken. The branches have now gone, with only the trunk remaining. Its origins are unknown, but by 1777 it appeared on maps as the Great Oak. It was still alive in 1860, and had a girth of almost 30ft and a height of over 80ft. Another tree known as the Young Oak was planted nearby in 1863.

**Castle Hedingham
St James Street c1965**
C238020
Here we see a wide road with little moving traffic. Many of the buildings remain, almost unchanged. The post office stands on the right, with a stamp machine on the wall outside. The massive keep of the castle that gives the village its name attracts many visitors.

**Sible Hedingham
The Almshouses,
Swan Street 1953**

S276008

The almshouses are in
the foreground on the
right-hand side. A
plaque above the door
bearing the date 1884
records that they were
built in memory of
Maria Webster,
'dedicated and
declared free for ever'.
The Swan Inn, with its
tall chimney and man
working on a ladder, is
near the bottom of the
hill.

Eastwards to the Coast

Halstead
Bridge Street c1955 H168009
The market here was established in 1251. This road takes its name
from the bridge over the River Colne, visible in the foreground of
the picture. The scene is little changed, apart from the style and
number of cars and the increase in pedestrian traffic. The Bull
Hotel, with its massive chimneys, dominates this part of the road.

Halstead, St Andrew's Church, High Street c1955 H168012
Much of the church dates from the 14th century, but the old west tower fell down and was rebuilt in 1850;
further restoration followed. Although the shops now have new proprietors, the upper parts of the buildings are
unchanged. Towards the end of the row, a policeman stops to talk to a cyclist.

Earls Colne, Church Hill c1960 E67022
The village takes its name from the river that flows through the valley and from the earls of the de Vere family. This photograph is typical of the type of rural scene to be found in Essex. The church of St Andrew dominates the gently rising land. Although much of the building was rebuilt in Victorian times, the tower dates from 1535. The decoration includes the mullet (or star), the badge of the de Veres.

White Colne, From the Green c1955 W194011
This road makes its way down to a bridge over the River Colne, from which this village also takes its name. There is a timeless quality about this picture: apart from some painting, the houses have changed little in the years since the photograph was taken. Note the unusual porch on the timber-framed house. A lone cyclist pedals by.

White Colne, Colneford House c1955 W194016
Colneford House stands on Colneford Hill and overlooks the green we see in W194011. The walls of this fine old house are covered in superb pargeting. Over the central porch is the date 1685.

Manningtree, High Street c1955 M127025
This is a quiet town on the south bank of the River Stour, at the point where it begins to widen into the estuary. In the High Street there are a few parked cars, but no pedestrians, apart from the two women and a child in the doorway on the right. That house is now a shop, and the large building with the clock has been replaced with new houses. We can see the Crown Hotel towards the end of the road on the left.

Bradfield, The Heath c1955 B810019
A little further east from Mistley is the village of Bradfield. Here we see C Sparkes' corner shop; there are large advertisements fixed to the wall, and one for Wills' Woodbines attached to the fence. There is also a post box. This building stands on the corner of Barrack Street, and is now a private house.

◀ **Mistley, The Quay c1955** M131006
Built on the estuary of the Stour, and close to Manningtree, this is a fascinating town. The large buildings behind the barge are maltings, now being converted into living accommodation. This is still a working port where seabirds abound.

▼ **Harwich, The Recreation Ground c1960** H150019
The building with the tower is known as Low Lighthouse, although it has now been converted into the Maritime Museum. Built in 1818, it replaced an earlier wooden structure. Beach huts line the edge of the green. The small shop on the right still opens to serve summer visitors.

◀ **Harwich Harbour Road c1965**
H150025
As we approach the town, it is possible to see cranes rising above the waterfront of this busy port. Harbour Road is close to the sea. Both the Angel and the next building are clad in weatherboard. Further down the road on the right is the Globe Hotel.

Dovercourt, The Beach and New Promenade c1955 D51016
Dovercourt lies south of Harwich. Here we have a busy scene, with most of those enjoying the beach placing their deckchairs close to the sea wall. This is a sandy beach, ideal for making sand castles. The lighthouse tower was restored between 1983 and 1988.

Dovercourt, High Street c1955 D51028
This busy High Street scene shows many well known shop names. The Home and Colonial (right) was a popular grocery store. Boots advertises its developing and printing service (left), and Stead and Simpson, the shoe store, is next door. Most shops still have awnings, ready to pull down if the sun gets strong. Leons Café, in the distance on the right, offers luncheons and teas.

Thorpe-le-Soken, The Village c1955 T253003
Here we have an interesting village street. Wares from the small shop on the right spill out onto the pavement, and among other commodities it advertises petrol! A garage stands on the left with a hose stretching out towards the road. The church of St Michael, in the background, was largely rebuilt in the 19th century, but the west tower dates from Tudor times.

Walton-on-the-Naze, The Coronation Camping Ground c1955 W18006
At this time camping holidays were extremely popular. Both touring and permanent caravans were used. A shop like the one on the left was vital to supply the needs of the holidaymakers when many people travelled by bus or train. The town is well known for its fossil-bearing cliffs.

▼ **Frinton-on-Sea, The Beach c1955** F53020
The visitor approaching Frinton by road has to pass over a level crossing. Here we see the wide expanse of sandy beach, ideal for family holidays. Above the huts there is a greensward between the beach and the road.

▼ **Frinton-on-Sea, Connaught Avenue and the Free Church c1955**
F53015
The Free Church, with its imposing clock tower, lies to the right of this picture. This is a busy road for both cars and pedestrians. In the foreground, in front of the Galleon (selling confectionery) and Constance Williams's shop, is a small garden with a telephone box.

▲ **Holland-on-Sea
The Bowling Green
c1955** H177044
This bowling green is close to the sea. Bowls was, for many years, regarded as a sport for older men, but it is now popular with both women and young men. In this picture we see senior citizens enjoying the game, all wearing caps to protect their heads. A single-decker bus can be seen in the background.

◄ **Clacton-on-Sea**
Central Promenade c1936
C107007
Although Great Clacton was long-established as a medieval market village, the seaside town did not really develop until late in the 19th century. By the years just before the Second World War, it had become a thriving town attracting many holiday visitors. Here we see crowds flocking around the pier with its swimming pool and theatre. Cars were gaining in importance by this time.

**Clacton-on-Sea
The Pier c1960**
C107062
This sandy beach was obviously popular with both children and adults. A Punch and Judy show always drew the crowds (centre), and many visitors enjoyed a trip on one of the pleasure boats. On the pier there is an amusement park, with the Big Dipper taking pride of place.

▼ Jaywick, Brooklands Avenue c1960 J4040

Jaywick is divided from Clacton by a golf course and a Martello Tower. This became a popular holiday area after Jaywick Farm was sold following the farming recession of the 1930s. The land was sold in small plots, and the area became a bungalow township. Here we see holidaymakers enjoying their time by the sea.

▼ Jaywick, Chester Chalets c1955 J4010

This is one of the larger chalets with a garage at the side. Some of the much-loved deckchairs of the period are leaning against the wall, with bicycles for transport. In many parts of Jaywick the chalets are in narrow lanes, but here we see a grassed site with other chalets and a caravan on the left of the picture.

▲ Jaywick, A 'B'-Type Bungalow c1955 J4026

Most of the permanent chalets were raised on piers, like this one where a young boy smiles for the camera. In 1953 the sea broke through the defences, causing great distress and some loss of life. Since then the sea walls have been raised, making it impossible to get sea views from the low-lying chalets.

◀ **St Osyth, The Ferry Point Clear Bay c1955**
S38055
Here we see a sailor about to launch his rowing boat. The town is built close to St Osyth's creek, and takes its name from the wife of a 7th-century Essex king. The remains of a superb abbey are to be found close by.

St Osyth, Point Clear Bay from the Martello Tower c1955 S38063
Martello Towers were built in the time of Napoleon to guard the coast. This photograph gives an excellent view of the chalets built close to the sea wall; they are raised, leaving space for boats, cars or general storage underneath. Holiday entertainment often included Bingo.

Fingringhoe, The Whalebone Inn c1960 F27001
This is a pretty, quiet village close to the Roman River. The Whalebone remains virtually unchanged from the time when this photograph was taken. Nearby is St Michael's church and the school. The church has a large square tower striped horizontally.

Wivenhoe, High Street c1960 W160027
Wivenhoe is situated on the River Colne. Here we have a view of the High Street at a quiet time. In the foreground is the railway, and further back stands the church of St Mary the Virgin. The Grosvenor Hotel on the right has now gone, and the building houses shops. Today the University of Essex campus is to the north-west of the town.

Elmstead Market, The Bowling Green c1965 E69015
The inn is now closed; at one time there was a bowling green nearby from which it may have taken its name. Outside stands an AA patrol van. The house on the right is now described as Maltravers, '18th-century restaurant'. Beth Chatto's well-known garden can be found on the edge of the village.

Colchester, Old Houses, East Street c1955 C136001

Colchester is often described as Britain's oldest recorded town - this was a town of vital importance to the Romans. In this photograph Charles Brown & Sons advertise the sale of linoleum, rugs, floorcloth, mats and matting. A workman digging a hole in the road attracts the attention of mothers who pause with their prams. The timber-framed building close to the bridge is known as the Old Siege House.

Colchester, The Red Lion Hotel c1960 C136038

The imposing Red Lion Hotel overlooks a busy market scene. Kendall, the well-known store stocking umbrellas and rainwear, can be seen on the right. By this time the style of prams had become sleeker than those in C136001, as we can see from those displayed in the window above the wireless shop.

North of the Blackwater, West of the Colne Estuary

West Mersea
Old Mersea c1960 W190045
To reach West Mersea it is necessary to pass over the Strood,
a causeway which is liable to flood at high tide. These
attractive weatherboarded houses still stand. Once Mrs
Cudmore ran the tea shop, offering home-made cakes.

Tollesbury
The Square c1955
T117014
The wide square has
parking space in the
middle; in the left-hand
corner stands the King's
Head hotel. Opposite is
Roebuck House, which
dates from the late
14th century. The shop
is now a private house.

◀ **Kelvedon, High Street c1955** K59004
Apart from an increase of traffic and the removal of the creeper growing over Knights Templars Terrace on the left, this scene has changed little. The White Hart (right) is believed to date back at least to 1720; it is now no longer an inn.

Tiptree, The Windmill c1955 T116015

This town is noted for its strawberry fields and the Wilkins jam factory. The tower windmill is currently without its sails. There are tales that it was once used as a smugglers' hiding place for contraband brought up the River Blackwater.

Great Braxted The Village c1960 G94003

The DuCane family, merchants of Huguenot descent, bought a large estate near the village in 1751. Their house, built in 1670, underwent extensive alterations in 1752-56. The DuCane Arms takes its name from the family, and stands on the site of an earlier alehouse.

Wickham Bishops Blue Mill c1960

W196015

This delightful mill is to be found on the River Blackwater. Few can pass over the hump-backed bridge without pausing to get a better view. In rural areas, mills like this were vital for farmers who needed their wheat ground; both water and windmills were used in Essex.

**Great Totham
Maldon Road c1965**
G99004
Great Totham Garage is
still to be found behind
the shop in Maldon
Road. In this picture,
motorists stop to fill up
with Regent petrol at
the pumps - these have
now gone, but apart
from that little has
changed over the years.

◀ **Heybridge
The Old Ship and the
Jolly Sailors Inn c1955**
H174024
In 1793 the Basin at
Heybridge was dug out
to provide access from
the Chelmer and
Blackwater Canal to the
sea via the sea lock. This
is a popular area for
boating, and here we
see two of the inns
much used by those
who have enjoyed a day
afloat - the Old Ship to
the left, and the Jolly
Sailor facing the camera.

**Heybridge
The Children's Boating
Pool c1955** H174017
Here we see a large
caravan park, very popular
at this time. For children
the boating pool would
have been an added
attraction, and parents
could watch from the
pavilion balcony as they
enjoyed a cup of tea.
Clark's, the well-known
shellfish supplier, traded
from the small shop.

**Maldon, The River
Blackwater c1955**
M12020
A great battle took place in
Maldon in 991: the
Vikings invaded the
mainland after crossing a
causeway that can still be
seen at low tide. Here we
see a busy waterfront area.
Many of the remaining
Thames barges are
moored at Maldon.

**Maldon
Market Hill Corner
c1955** M12034
This medieval flint tower
belonged to St Peter's
church. However, it now
simply serves as the
vestibule to the public
library. This replaced the
church building in 1704,
under the instruction of
Dr Thomas Plume.

Witham
Newland Street c1955
W119010
Awnings protect the shop fronts on this sunny day. A wide variety of building styles can be seen in the row on the right of the road. Apart from a change in function of many of the shops, this road has altered little over the years. The Spread Eagle in the foreground is dated 1300.

◀ **Witham, Church Street
c1965** W119048
The White Horse (right)
has undergone some
changes over the years.
In the centre of the
picture stands the forge,
which is believed to
date back over 670
years, although it is
thought that horses and
ponies were shod here
long before that.

◄ Witham, The White Hart and Newland Street c1955

W119008

Here the photographer has moved closer to the White Hart, with its dominant sign. The painted traffic light supports would be hard to miss, but they are set very near to the edge of the kerb. The newsagent on the right displays his advertisement boards on the pavement. Next door C H Gallant, the butcher, announces the sale of prime Canterbury lamb.

▼ Terling, The Street c1960

T110018

This rambling village is a mixture of the old and the new. Here we see Terling Stores and Post Office. This has always been a meeting place for local shoppers - here a mother shows off her young child. Parts of this building are claimed to go back at least to the 14th century.

◄ Little Waltham The Village c1965

L158008

This pretty village has changed little over the years, apart from an increase in traffic - here the Bell Hotel claims to have a large car park. The house behind the large tree, now felled, has attractive pargeting and dates from the 17th century.

The South-East

Hatfield Peverel
The Green c1960 H173006
Until the early years of the 20th century, a thriving brewery, which
was run by the Brown family, stood on the green. The large house
on the left is Brewery House, and behind the post box is Brewery
Barn with Brewery Cottages close by. The white building at the
end of this row is Ann Cottage, which bears the date 1580.

Little Baddow, Paper Mill Lock, the River Chelmer c1960 L153011
This is part of the Chelmer and Blackwater Navigation. The lock was built between 1793 and 1797, and the principal engineer was John Rennie. Although the lock gates are changed at regular intervals, the original lock chamber remains. The bridge in the background replaced an earlier wooden structure.

▼ **Little Baddow, The Best Kept Village Sign c1960** L153017
This sign was set up in front of the Little Baddow Memorial Hall. The swords on the county coat of arms are seaxes, the short swords or sword knives used by the Saxons, which may in fact have been straight rather than curved. The cutting edges face upwards.

▼ **Danbury, Eve's Corner c1965** D1004
This tranquil scene shows the village pond with the reflection of the houses on its surface. Danbury is built on high ground, and the spire of St John the Baptist's church can be seen from a considerable distance.

▲ **Chelmsford, Moulsham Street c1950** C73028
Moulsham Street has now been cut in two by the building of Parkway. It is a continuation of the High Street, which we see in C73044. Although only fifteen years separate these two photographs, here motorised traffic seems to cause little problem to those walking and cycling in the road. Loveday and Son, the watchmaker and jeweller's, complete with the clock, still survives on the corner of Baddow Street (left), but the International Stores (right) and many of the other shops have now changed hands.

◀ **Chelmsford, High Street c1955** C73044

Chelmsford has been the county town of Essex since at least the 13th century. Here we see the busy High Street in the days long before it was pedestrianised. The large building at the end of the road is the impressive Shire Hall, built 1789-1791; it serves as the courthouse. The upper stories of the buildings on the right are little changed, although many of the shops are under new ownership.

Great Baddow, The White Horse and the Pump c1965 G92014
The White Horse stands in the High Street with a car park at the rear. Note the tall, brick-built chimneys. On the grass in front of the hotel is a pump and a trough. The hotel has now extended into the next building with the porch.

Galleywood, The Parade c1965 G90013
This development is known as Galleywood Village Shops. The shops have changed little with the passing years, and at least two still have these distinctively styled awnings. High prams with large wheels were popular at this time.

East Hanningfield, The Post Office c1960 E255001

In a small village, the post office and general store was always important. This one states boldly that telegrams could be dispatched. A letterbox is set in the wall. This building is now a private house.

East Hanningfield, The Windmill c1960 E255009

East Hanningfield is some way from the large reservoir that dominates the area. Here we see the Windmill public house, where Truman's beer was sold. The building apparently dates from the early years of the 18th century. The small notice on the signpost discourages coaches.

▼ **Mayland, The River c1965** M130060
Mayland is a flat marshy area on Mayland Creek, which empties into the River Blackwater. Although rather bleak in winter, in summer it is a busy centre for sailing. The Maylandsea Sailing Club is on the right of the picture.

▼ **Tillingham, The Square c1955** T115008
Weatherboarded cottages stand to the left. The large building on the same side is the Fox and Hounds. W Kemp's shop, on the right, is now a private house. Behind the photographer is the ancient church of St Nicholas.

▲ **Burnham-on-Crouch High Street c1950**
B325018
This wide High Street has altered little over the years, although the proprietors of many of the shops have changed. The octagonal clock tower was added to St Mary's School in 1877 in memory of Laban Sweeting - the building has now been adapted for living accommodation. Over the top of the windows of the second building on the left are the words 'Standard Tea Warehouse', its former use.

◀ **Althorne, Main Road
c1955** A107004
This village lies close to the River Crouch. We can see the sign for the Black Lion hotel on the last building in the row. The weatherboarded cottages nearby are known as Black Lion Cottages. The two shops in the foreground display advertisements for Oxo, Lifeguard soap and Lamberts teas, and many other products.

Wallasea Bay, The Ferry Pier c1965 W187013
In this remote corner of Essex, close to the Wardroom, the Wallasea Bay Ferry plies its trade. The floating jetty we see here has disappeared, to be replaced by a more substantial structure, but large chunks of the original wood still litter the marshes. Across the River Crouch lie Burnham and Creeksea. On the left of the picture we can see three fuel pumps with a wind sock flying above.

Shoeburyness, The Children's Boating Pool c1955 S275019
Here children tentatively set out on a journey across the boating lake at Shoeburyness. This playground area was close to the sea. Miniature golf was another attraction, with a round of eighteen holes costing the princely sum of 9d.

Shoeburyness, Shoebury Hall Farm Camp c1955 S275035
Shoebury, a garrison town to the east of Southend-on-Sea, attracted many holidaymakers who enjoyed camping. This site opened in 1932 and was owned by Captain Townend; at first it was used by holidaymakers in tents, but later caravans became important. The site warden was Mr Jim Hooper.

Southend-on-Sea, The Boating Lake c1950 S155006
The Boating Lake, to the east of the pier, was always popular with children. Families would often hire deckchairs to sit and picnic beside the pool. Many of the well-known shops of the area face the sea. A walk along the promenade has been enjoyed by generations of visitors to the town.

Southend-on-Sea, The Boating Lake c1950 S155020
This photograph looks west beside the boating pool, with the Palace Hotel dominating the scene. Built in 1904, this fine hotel served as Queen Mary's Naval Hospital during the First World War. At the top of Pier Hill is Royal Terrace, so named because it was here that the Princesses Caroline and Charlotte stayed when visiting the town early in the 19th century.

Southend-on-Sea, The Golden Hind and the Pier c1950 S155033
This replica of Sir Francis Drake's flagship was built 1947-48. Standing beside the pier, it housed Louis Tussaud's Waxworks, a major attraction in this area. On the left of the picture we can see the boating lake.

Hadleigh, The Castle c1960 H167016
Originally, Hubert de Burg was granted a licence to construct this castle in 1250, but it was completely rebuilt in the time of Edward III. Now little remains of the massive structure that once guarded the coast to the west of Leigh-on-Sea. The building fell into disrepair, especially in the 16th century. The castle was immortalised by John Constable.

▼ **Rochford, The Hall c1955** R226025
Of the original mansion built in the mid 16th century, only the corner tower survives. This substantial building now houses the Rochford Hundred Golf Club. Ann Boleyn had links with this ancient town.

▼ **Thundersley, The Weir Roundabout c1960** T113031
This roundabout was once a notorious black spot for traffic jams on the route from Southend to London; now it has been replaced by an underpass. The Weir Hotel was well used by motorists, as we can see from the many cars parked outside.

▲ **South Benfleet High Street c1960**
S278071
The Hoy & Helmet, on the left, was originally built in the 15th century, with later extensions. A hoy was a broad sailing boat used to transport farming produce. The word 'Helmet' was added to the name in 1922, this being the hard on which the boats were drawn up. This was a centre for smuggling in the 19th century, with tunnels under what is now the car park.

◀ **Canvey Island**
The Beach c1955 C237020
In the 1950s seaside towns had a revival, and were often very crowded. Hired deckchairs occupy much of the space on the beach. Although many of the older people enjoying the sun are well wrapped up, the boy on the right digs happily without a shirt.

**Canvey Island
The Beach c1960**
C237086
In 1953 devastating
floods cost many
islanders their homes,
and lives were lost.
A raised sea wall now
protects the land
behind from
encroachment by the
sea, but is being used
as a backrest by some
of the holidaymakers.

Looking South

Great Tarpots
Tarpots Hall c1955 G98004
Dated 1928, the upper part of Tarpots Hall was used by 1341
Thames Estuary Squadron ATC. The lower storey contained a
dance floor, popular with young people at the time. The building,
including Tarpots Bakery (left), has now been redeveloped.

Pitsea, The Shops c1955 P145004
Pitsea lies to the north of Bowers Marshes. Since the development of Basildon in the second half of the 20th century, much of its earlier identity has been lost, with many older buildings disappearing under new developments. Photographs like this give a reminder of what the town once looked like. The store marked Electricity proclaims its summer sale.

Corringham, High Street c1950 C243013
In this picture we see a parade of shops with bay-windowed accommodation above. Note the awnings protecting goods displayed in the windows from fading in the glare of the sun. Corringham is close to Coryton, known for its oil refineries.

◄ **Stanford-le-Hope
The Green c1960**

S258025
These shops face the
small bus shelter in the
centre of S258082.
Above G W Ager's
'Complete Outfitters' is
an advertisement for
Dunlop boots. The
impressive war
memorial records the
names of the dead of
both World Wars of the
20th century.

◄ Stanford-le-Hope
The View from the
Church Tower c1960
S258082

The large house next to Lloyds Bank was once a doctor's surgery, and it is now a public house known as the Inn on the Green. This interesting photograph also gives a good view of the war memorial and the edge of the churchyard with its lych-gate.

▼ Horndon-on-the-Hill
High Street, North End
c1960 H178002

The weatherboarded cottages on the left are known as Halls Row Cottages. The school, erected in 1847, was a National School. On the opposite side of the road, behind the thatched cottage, is the Wesleyan Methodist Chapel, built in 1890.

◄ Tilbury, The Thames
c1960 T114010

This is a busy dockside area on the north bank of the River Thames, where tall cranes pierce the skyline. Here we see the 'Vruburgh' from Rotterdam, and dock buildings lining the waterfront. Nearby is the historic Tilbury Fort.

◀ **Grays, The Children's Boating Pool c1955**
G85004
Boating pools could be found in many parks in the 1950s. Here a number of children show interest in the launching of the boat. Behind the wall, lined with seats, is the River Thames.

Tilbury, The Riverside c1960 T114034

Before the building of the Dartford tunnels and the Queen Elizabeth II bridge, the Tilbury ferry was an important means of crossing the Thames for motorists in this part of Essex. Now only a passenger ferry functions. Cranes rise in the background.

Grays, The Parade c1955 G85035

A busy parade of shops with distinctive gables line the road at this point. Several prams can be seen outside, and a child rides happily on the pavement on a tricycle. The row of shops remains, although the proprietors have changed. The road outside has changed too - the grass verge has disappeared under a road-widening scheme. The road is now the very busy A1013, formerly the A13.

Purfleet, Botany Cottages c1955

P148003

This row of twelve cottages bears a large crest in the centre with the date 1905. At Purfleet a thick fold of chalk rises above the River Thames, and extensive quarrying has been carried out in the area.

▼ **Purfleet, London Road c1955** P148004

As the road approaches the level crossing, we can see a signal box and a foot bridge - in recent years the signal box has been demolished. The row of cottages on the left is known as Station Terrace, with the post office close to the camera with a post box and stamp machine set into the wall. Advertisements for Player's and Craven A cigarettes are prominently displayed.

▼ **Aveley, High Street c1955** A110003

The Crown and Anchor (left) was once a private house; parts of the building are believed to date from the 14th and 15th centuries. The shop beyond, advertising Vitbe bread, has now been replaced by a Quick Save store. Note the motorcycle and sidecar outside yet another shop advertising cigarettes.

▲ **Aveley, The Cricket Pitch c1955** A110006
Here we see a summer cricket match in full swing. The sporting facilities and club rooms were taken over by the London Fire Brigade Welfare Fund in the 1980s. It is still a very well used sports and social club.

◄ **Aveley, The Ship Hotel c1955** A110034
The imposing Ship Hotel appears to have been a popular meeting place. It has links with the past, and a blocked tunnel is said to have led to St Michael's church that stands nearby. Where A Fryer once sold boots and shoes (left), there is now a private house.

▼ **South Ockendon, The Village c1955** S280019
This scene is now much changed. However, the war memorial
remains on the village green as a tribute to those who died in both
the major wars of the 20th century. To the right of the photographer
is the interesting church of St Nicholas with its round west tower.

▼ **Bulphan, The School c1955** B323007
Built in 1864, Bulphan Church of England Primary School is typical
of many small village schools; it is still in use. The church of St Mary
is nearby. The village itself is small and quiet.

▲ **Laindon, The Fortune
of War Hotel c1960**
L150033
The Fortune of War
stands on a roundabout
on the busy Southend
Arterial Road. It is an
impressive building, and
always attracted many
customers. Repairs are
apparently being carried
out to the roof, and the
opening time is clearly
displayed to attract the
attention of passing
motorists. The large pipes
on the right were no
doubt ready for major
road works.

◀ **Wickford, High Street c1950** W195003
This busy street is crowded with shoppers, although the road is still fairly free from traffic. Awnings protect the shop fronts and the goods displayed in the windows. The town has grown considerably in recent years.

▼ **Wickford, Nevendon Village c1955** W195011

Once again the village store and post office displays advertisements for cigarettes, this time for Craven A and Gold Flake. This is now a much widened and busy road where no one would any longer be rash enough to walk in the centre.

▼ **Billericay, High Street c1965** B319058

One of the highly successful Austin Minis is parked in the foreground. The International Stores was popular for groceries; also, note the many newspaper and magazine advertisements outside Martins, the newsagent's shop (right). Horsnell Bros functions as both an ironmongers and a greengrocers. The brick tower of St Mary Magdalene's church dates from the 15th century.

▲ **Shenfield, Market Place c1955** S109016

Market Place is now known as Hutton Road, but the row of shops shown here is easily recognisable today. Guthrie's Garage is still trading, although the road outside has a constant stream of traffic, unlike the quiet scene shown in this photograph.

Brentwood, High Street c1955 B198002

Brentwood stands on the Roman road that ran from London to Chelmsford and Colchester. This view was taken looking west. Note the running board on the car in the foreground, and the awnings protecting the shop fronts. Outside the Sir Charles Napier public house stands a telephone box (centre right). On the wall next door is a large Guinness advertisement.

Ingatestone, The Hall, the Gateway and the Courtyard c1955 I10013
This beautiful Tudor house is owned by the Petre family. Sir William Petre moved here in 1539, and the Hall was built over the next ten years. Above this arch there is an impressive clock tower.

Blackmore, The Green c1960 B320010
Blackmore is a typically well kept Essex village. The war memorial lists the names of members of the armed forces who lost their lives, especially in the First World War. On the far side of the green, the duck pond is a haven for wildlife.

To the West of Chelmsford

Navestock
The Church c1955 N263058
This rural scene shows the church of St Thomas the Apostle.
The belfry, built in an interesting style found in several Essex
churches, has a sloping tiled roof placed between the various
stages of the tower. This is surmounted by a spire. The earliest
parts of the building date from the 11th and 12th centuries.

▼ **Ongar, Chipping Ongar, High Street c1955** O19001
The house on the right stands on the corner of Castle Street, a reminder that the town once had a Norman castle. Murphy televisions and radios are proudly advertised on the banner (left). The complete absence of cars reminds us of a much quieter time in the history of the town.

▼ **Ongar, Chipping Ongar, High Street c1955** O19002
This is another view of the High Street, although here the road is much wider. The London Co-operative Society shop can be seen on the right. These stores were well used at this time - shoppers could also collect their dividend points. Single-decker buses (right) were widely used in rural and semi-rural areas.

▲ **Writtle, The Village c1955** W154009
Although Writtle is close to Chelmsford, it still manages to retain a village atmosphere. Here we see a large, attractive duck pond. The shop with the awning still serves as the post office. Behind the war memorial stands a weatherboarded cottage.

◀ **Great Waltham
Chelmsford Road c1965**

G101009

The Fiat garage seen here is typical of the period; Castrol and Regent petrol are advertised, and so are Green Shield Stamps - when enough of these had been collected, they could be exchanged for a wide variety of goods. Once again weatherboard has been used on the side of one of the houses. The church of St Mary and St Lawrence stands in the background.

Pleshey, The View from the Church Tower c1965 P146010 This great castle mound is perhaps best seen from the top of church tower: it is a fine example of a motte and bailey. The castle itself has long since disappeared - it was of timber, and dated from early Norman times. A brick bridge over the moat remains.

High Easter, The Church and the Punch Bowl c1960 H175012
Here we can see a cellar hatch in the pavement where beer barrels would once have been delivered. The Punch Bowl has been altered and restored and turned into a restaurant since this photograph was taken. In the background stands the church of St Mary the Virgin - its flint tower dates from the 15th century.

Fyfield, Dunmow Road c1950 F80012
This quiet road has now been widened, and there is little sign of the water-filled ditch. However, the property on the left and the barn projecting towards the road remain unchanged. The delivery van, complete with running board (right), would have been a welcome lifeline in a rural area like this.

Hatfield Broad Oak, St Mary's Church c1965 H171015
A Benedictine priory was founded here in 1135; many of the monastic buildings were destroyed during the Reformation. The plaque on the second cottage on the left bears the initials 'CBAM' and is dated 1708. In the north-west corner of the parish lies the ancient Hatfield Forest.

◄ **Hatfield Heath**
The Post Office c1965
H172011
Once again we see a
typical weatherboarded
Essex cottage. Further
along the row is an
attractive thatched
house. Horses outside
the post office give a
rural air to this scene.

◀ **Hatfield Heath
The Clipped Hedge
Tea Rooms c1960**

H172008
This beautiful thatched
building is now known
as Clipped Hedge
Cottage. The pond has
been much reduced in
size: a road has been
built over part of it, and
the land behind has
been used to build a
small housing
development.

▼ **Old Harlow, Churchgate Street
c1965** O43013
The area known as Churchgate
Street lies close to Old Harlow, and
has the air of a quiet village. The
beautiful timber-framed house,
beside the lych-gate leading into the
church of St Mary the Virgin, has an
inscription over the door dated
1630. It states that the house was
given by Julian, the wife of Alex
Stafford Esq, for 'the habitation of
two poor widows of this Parish'.

◀ **Harlow, The River
Stort c1955** H22012
The idea for Harlow
New Town dates from
the late 1940s. It was
seen as a way to relieve
some of the congestion
in London. Through this
area runs the River Stort,
which also forms one of
the boundary lines for
the county. The river has
always attracted both
visitors and residents;
here we see a busy
summer day when many
have arrived by bicycle.
Good paths can be used
for walking or cycling.

Great Parndon, The Cock Inn c1960 G97004
This old building has undergone a number of changes over the years. Once a large elm stood close by, but this was lost during the problems with Dutch elm disease. The area around is now built up and lies in the outskirts of Harlow.

Roydon, High Street c1955 R229007
Close to the county boundary, Roydon retains a timeless air. Here we see the White Horse, partly weatherboarded, with small, brick-built cottages beyond. The railings around the garden on the left apparently survived the war years, when many were removed.

Roydon, The Old House c1955 R229019
The road outside this attractive timber-framed and weatherboarded house has changed little over the years. Note the impressive chimneys, both on the side and in the centre of the building.

Waltham Abbey, The Old Gateway c1955 W14005
This ruined gateway belonged to the 14th-century Augustinian abbey of Holy Cross. The smaller archway was for pedestrian traffic, whilst the larger one was meant for wheeled vehicles. In the background we can see the tower of the abbey church.

**Waltham Abbey
The Welsh Harp
c1955** W14014
This picturesque,
timber-framed inn,
formerly known simply
as the Harp, has stood
on this site since the
15th or 16th century.
A passageway leads
through to the
churchyard. Part of the
building may once have
been the priest's house.

Epping, High Street c1955 E38019

This is a wide street, narrowing towards the end. The ancient Black Lion Hotel stands on the left. Awnings protect many of the shop fronts. Ye Olde Oak Hotel on the right still stands, but has changed its use - the cockerel sign remains, however.

Epping, The View from Upshire c1955 E38031

For many years, Epping Forest has been a favourite place for family outings and picnics. This is but a small remnant of the ancient Forest of Essex that existed in pre-historic times. Both Henry VIII and Elizabeth I hunted here. However, in 1882 Queen Victoria announced that the forest should be for the use and enjoyment of her people for all time.

North Weald, The King's Head c1955 N68006
Parts of this beautiful old building date back to the middle years of the 16th century. Much of the woodwork came from old ships' timbers - this was at a time when newer wood was taken for the building of warships. During World War II the Kings Head was a popular watering-hole for airmen based at the nearby North Weald airfield.

Loughton, Lopping Hall c1955 L106032
Behind Hutchin's pharmacy we can see the tower of Lopping Hall. A blue plaque recalls that this was built in 1883 out of compensation paid for the loss of tree-lopping rights in Epping Forest. This followed the Epping Forest Act of 1878 which stopped pollarding, but grazing rights were continued.

Abridge, The Village c1955 A106012
Here we have a quiet village scene, little changed by time. The weatherboarded building on the right has served as the post office for many years, and the white building on the left is the Blue Boar. Note the style of prams used by the ladies chatting on the right.

Chigwell, Brook Parade c1950 C88009
Here we see a typical shopping parade of the 1950s. It includes two banks, a newsagent's and a garage. The Midland Bank, on the corner of the row, now bears the name HSBC. The whole parade has been extended to the right.

Chigwell, The Swimming Pool, Grange Farm Centre c1955 C88022
We complete our journey around Essex in Chigwell, with this view of an open-air swimming pool. These were popular places for family outings on sunny days in the 1950s and 60s. Here young children splash in the paddling pool, while others are more adventurous in the main pool. Sad to say, this centre is no more, and the pool has been filled in. However, apparently there are plans for future recreational and conservation activities on the site.

Index

Frith Book Co Titles

www.francisfrith.co.uk

The Frith Book Company publishes over 100 new titles each year. A selection of those currently available are listed below. For latest catalogue please contact Frith Book Co.

Town Books 96 pages, approx 100 photos. County and Themed Books 128 pages, approx 150 photos (unless specified). All titles hardback laminated case and jacket except those indicated pb (paperback)

Amersham, Chesham & Rickmansworth (pb)			Derby (pb)	1-85937-367-4	£9.99
	1-85937-340-2	£9.99	Derbyshire (pb)	1-85937-196-5	£9.99
Ancient Monuments & Stone Circles	1-85937-143-4	£17.99	Devon (pb)	1-85937-297-x	£9.99
Aylesbury (pb)	1-85937-227-9	£9.99	Dorset (pb)	1-85937-269-4	£9.99
Bakewell	1-85937-113-2	£12.99	Dorset Churches	1-85937-172-8	£17.99
Barnstaple (pb)	1-85937-300-3	£9.99	Dorset Coast (pb)	1-85937-299-6	£9.99
Bath (pb)	1-85937419-0	£9.99	Dorset Living Memories	1-85937-210-4	£14.99
Bedford (pb)	1-85937-205-8	£9.99	Down the Severn	1-85937-118-3	£14.99
Berkshire (pb)	1-85937-191-4	£9.99	Down the Thames (pb)	1-85937-278-3	£9.99
Berkshire Churches	1-85937-170-1	£17.99	Down the Trent	1-85937-311-9	£14.99
Blackpool (pb)	1-85937-382-8	£9.99	Dublin (pb)	1-85937-231-7	£9.99
Bognor Regis (pb)	1-85937-431-x	£9.99	East Anglia (pb)	1-85937-265-1	£9.99
Bournemouth	1-85937-067-5	£12.99	East London	1-85937-080-2	£14.99
Bradford (pb)	1-85937-204-x	£9.99	East Sussex	1-85937-130-2	£14.99
Brighton & Hove(pb)	1-85937-192-2	£8.99	Eastbourne	1-85937-061-6	£12.99
Bristol (pb)	1-85937-264-3	£9.99	Edinburgh (pb)	1-85937-193-0	£8.99
British Life A Century Ago (pb)	1-85937-213-9	£9.99	England in the 1880s	1-85937-331-3	£17.99
Buckinghamshire (pb)	1-85937-200-7	£9.99	English Castles (pb)	1-85937-434-4	£9.99
Camberley (pb)	1-85937-222-8	£9.99	English Country Houses	1-85937-161-2	£17.99
Cambridge (pb)	1-85937-422-0	£9.99	Essex (pb)	1-85937-270-8	£9.99
Cambridgeshire (pb)	1-85937-420-4	£9.99	Exeter	1-85937-126-4	£12.99
Canals & Waterways (pb)	1-85937-291-0	£9.99	Exmoor	1-85937-132-9	£14.99
Canterbury Cathedral (pb)	1-85937-179-5	£9.99	Falmouth	1-85937-066-7	£12.99
Cardiff (pb)	1-85937-093-4	£9.99	Folkestone (pb)	1-85937-124-8	£9.99
Carmarthenshire	1-85937-216-3	£14.99	Glasgow (pb)	1-85937-190-6	£9.99
Chelmsford (pb)	1-85937-310-0	£9.99	Gloucestershire	1-85937-102-7	£14.99
Cheltenham (pb)	1-85937-095-0	£9.99	Great Yarmouth (pb)	1-85937-426-3	£9.99
Cheshire (pb)	1-85937-271-6	£9.99	Greater Manchester (pb)	1-85937-266-x	£9.99
Chester	1-85937-090-x	£12.99	Guildford (pb)	1-85937-410-7	£9.99
Chesterfield	1-85937-378-x	£9.99	Hampshire (pb)	1-85937-279-1	£9.99
Chichester (pb)	1-85937-228-7	£9.99	Hampshire Churches (pb)	1-85937-207-4	£9.99
Colchester (pb)	1-85937-188-4	£8.99	Harrogate	1-85937-423-9	£9.99
Cornish Coast	1-85937-163-9	£14.99	Hastings & Bexhill (pb)	1-85937-131-0	£9.99
Cornwall (pb)	1-85937-229-5	£9.99	Heart of Lancashire (pb)	1-85937-197-3	£9.99
Cornwall Living Memories	1-85937-248-1	£14.99	Helston (pb)	1-85937-214-7	£9.99
Cotswolds (pb)	1-85937-230-9	£9.99	Hereford (pb)	1-85937-175-2	£9.99
Cotswolds Living Memories	1-85937-255-4	£14.99	Herefordshire	1-85937-174-4	£14.99
County Durham	1-85937-123-x	£14.99	Hertfordshire (pb)	1-85937-247-3	£9.99
Croydon Living Memories	1-85937-162-0	£9.99	Horsham (pb)	1-85937-432-8	£9.99
Cumbria	1-85937-101-9	£14.99	Humberside	1-85937-215-5	£14.99
Dartmoor	1-85937-145-0	£14.99	Hythe, Romney Marsh & Ashford	1-85937-256-2	£9.99

Available from your local bookshop or from the publisher

Frith Book Co Titles (continued)

Ipswich (pb)	1-85937-424-7	£9.99	St Ives (pb)	1-85937415-8	£9.99
Ireland (pb)	1-85937-181-7	£9.99	Scotland (pb)	1-85937-182-5	£9.99
Isle of Man (pb)	1-85937-268-6	£9.99	Scottish Castles (pb)	1-85937-323-2	£9.99
Isles of Scilly	1-85937-136-1	£14.99	Sevenoaks & Tunbridge	1-85937-057-8	£12.99
Isle of Wight (pb)	1-85937-429-8	£9.99	Sheffield, South Yorks (pb)	1-85937-267-8	£9.99
Isle of Wight Living Memories	1-85937-304-6	£14.99	Shrewsbury (pb)	1-85937-325-9	£9.99
Kent (pb)	1-85937-189-2	£9.99	Shropshire (pb)	1-85937-326-7	£9.99
Kent Living Memories	1-85937-125-6	£14.99	Somerset	1-85937-153-1	£14.99
Lake District (pb)	1-85937-275-9	£9.99	South Devon Coast	1-85937-107-8	£14.99
Lancaster, Morecambe & Heysham (pb)	1-85937-233-3	£9.99	South Devon Living Memories	1-85937-168-x	£14.99
Leeds (pb)	1-85937-202-3	£9.99	South Hams	1-85937-220-1	£14.99
Leicester	1-85937-073-x	£12.99	Southampton (pb)	1-85937-427-1	£9.99
Leicestershire (pb)	1-85937-185-x	£9.99	Southport (pb)	1-85937-425-5	£9.99
Lincolnshire (pb)	1-85937-433-6	£9.99	Staffordshire	1-85937-047-0	£12.99
Liverpool & Merseyside (pb)	1-85937-234-1	£9.99	Stratford upon Avon	1-85937-098-5	£12.99
London (pb)	1-85937-183-3	£9.99	Suffolk (pb)	1-85937-221-x	£9.99
Ludlow (pb)	1-85937-176-0	£9.99	Suffolk Coast	1-85937-259-7	£14.99
Luton (pb)	1-85937-235-x	£9.99	Surrey (pb)	1-85937-240-6	£9.99
Maidstone	1-85937-056-x	£14.99	Sussex (pb)	1-85937-184-1	£9.99
Manchester (pb)	1-85937-198-1	£9.99	Swansea (pb)	1-85937-167-1	£9.99
Middlesex	1-85937-158-2	£14.99	Tees Valley & Cleveland	1-85937-211-2	£14.99
New Forest	1-85937-128-0	£14.99	Thanet (pb)	1-85937-116-7	£9.99
Newark (pb)	1-85937-366-6	£9.99	Tiverton (pb)	1-85937-178-7	£9.99
Newport, Wales (pb)	1-85937-258-9	£9.99	Torbay	1-85937-063-2	£12.99
Newquay (pb)	1-85937-421-2	£9.99	Truro	1-85937-147-7	£12.99
Norfolk (pb)	1-85937-195-7	£9.99	Victorian and Edwardian Cornwall	1-85937-252-x	£14.99
Norfolk Living Memories	1-85937-217-1	£14.99	Victorian & Edwardian Devon	1-85937-253-8	£14.99
Northamptonshire	1-85937-150-7	£14.99	Victorian & Edwardian Kent	1-85937-149-3	£14.99
Northumberland Tyne & Wear (pb)	1-85937-281-3	£9.99	Vic & Ed Maritime Album	1-85937-144-2	£17.99
North Devon Coast	1-85937-146-9	£14.99	Victorian and Edwardian Sussex	1-85937-157-4	£14.99
North Devon Living Memories	1-85937-261-9	£14.99	Victorian & Edwardian Yorkshire	1-85937-154-x	£14.99
North London	1-85937-206-6	£14.99	Victorian Seaside	1-85937-159-0	£17.99
North Wales (pb)	1-85937-298-8	£9.99	Villages of Devon (pb)	1-85937-293-7	£9.99
North Yorkshire (pb)	1-85937-236-8	£9.99	Villages of Kent (pb)	1-85937-294-5	£9.99
Norwich (pb)	1-85937-194-9	£8.99	Villages of Sussex (pb)	1-85937-295-3	£9.99
Nottingham (pb)	1-85937-324-0	£9.99	Warwickshire (pb)	1-85937-203-1	£9.99
Nottinghamshire (pb)	1-85937-187-6	£9.99	Welsh Castles (pb)	1-85937-322-4	£9.99
Oxford (pb)	1-85937-411-5	£9.99	West Midlands (pb)	1-85937-289-9	£9.99
Oxfordshire (pb)	1-85937-430-1	£9.99	West Sussex	1-85937-148-5	£14.99
Peak District (pb)	1-85937-280-5	£9.99	West Yorkshire (pb)	1-85937-201-5	£9.99
Penzance	1-85937-069-1	£12.99	Weymouth (pb)	1-85937-209-0	£9.99
Peterborough (pb)	1-85937-219-8	£9.99	Wiltshire (pb)	1-85937-277-5	£9.99
Piers	1-85937-237-6	£17.99	Wiltshire Churches (pb)	1-85937-171-x	£9.99
Plymouth	1-85937-119-1	£12.99	Wiltshire Living Memories	1-85937-245-7	£14.99
Poole & Sandbanks (pb)	1-85937-251-1	£9.99	Winchester (pb)	1-85937-428-x	£9.99
Preston (pb)	1-85937-212-0	£9.99	Windmills & Watermills	1-85937-242-2	£17.99
Reading (pb)	1-85937-238-4	£9.99	Worcester (pb)	1-85937-165-5	£9.99
Romford (pb)	1-85937-319-4	£9.99	Worcestershire	1-85937-152-3	£14.99
Salisbury (pb)	1-85937-239-2	£9.99	York (pb)	1-85937-199-x	£9.99
Scarborough (pb)	1-85937-379-8	£9.99	Yorkshire (pb)	1-85937-186-8	£9.99
St Albans (pb)	1-85937-341-0	£9.99	Yorkshire Living Memories	1-85937-166-3	£14.99

See Frith books on the internet www.francisfrith.co.uk

FRITH PRODUCTS & SERVICES

Francis Frith would doubtless be pleased to know that the pioneering publishing venture he started in 1860 still continues today. A hundred and forty years later, The Francis Frith Collection continues in the same innovative tradition and is now one of the foremost publishers of vintage photographs in the world. Some of the current activities include:

Interior Decoration

Today Frith's photographs can be seen framed and as giant wall murals in thousands of pubs, restaurants, hotels, banks, retail stores and other public buildings throughout the country. In every case they enhance the unique local atmosphere of the places they depict and provide reminders of gentler days in an increasingly busy and frenetic world.

Product Promotions

Frith products are used by many major companies to promote the sales of their own products or to reinforce their own history and heritage. Frith promotions have been used by Hovis bread, Courage beers, Scots Porage Oats, Colman's mustard, Cadbury's foods, Mellow Birds coffee, Dunhill pipe tobacco, Guinness, and Bulmer's Cider.

Genealogy and Family History

As the interest in family history and roots grows world-wide, more and more people are turning to Frith's photographs of Great Britain for images of the towns, villages and streets where their ancestors lived; and, of course, photographs of the churches and chapels where their ancestors were christened, married and buried are an essential part of every genealogy tree and family album.

Frith Products

All Frith photographs are available Framed or just as Mounted Prints and Posters (size 23 x 16 inches). These may be ordered from the address below. From time to time other products - Address Books, Calendars, Table Mats, etc - are available.

The Internet

Already twenty thousand Frith photographs can be viewed and purchased on the internet through the Frith websites and a myriad of partner sites.

For more detailed information on Frith companies and products, look at these sites:

www.francisfrith.co.uk
www.francisfrith.com
(for North American visitors)

See the complete list of Frith Books at:

www.francisfrith.co.uk

This web site is regularly updated with the latest list of publications from the Frith Book Company. If you wish to buy books relating to another part of the country that your local bookshop does not stock, you may purchase on-line.

For further information, trade, or author enquiries please contact us at the address below:
The Francis Frith Collection, Frith's Barn, Teffont, Salisbury, Wiltshire, England SP3 5QP.
Tel: +44 (0)1722 716 376 Fax: +44 (0)1722 716 881   Email: sales@francisfrith.co.uk

---

See Frith books on the internet www.francisfrith.co.uk

TO RECEIVE YOUR FREE MOUNTED PRINT

Mounted Print
Overall size 14 x 11 inches

Cut out this Voucher and return it with your remittance for £2.25 to cover postage and handling, to UK addresses. For overseas addresses please include £4.00 post and handling. Choose any photograph included in this book. Your SEPIA print will be A4 in size, and mounted in a cream mount with burgundy rule line, overall size 14 x 11 inches.

Order additional Mounted Prints at HALF PRICE (only £7.49 each*)

If there are further pictures you would like to order, possibly as gifts for friends and family, purchase them at half price (no additional postage and handling required).

Have your Mounted Prints framed*

For an additional £14.95 per print you can have your chosen Mounted Print framed in an elegant polished wood and gilt moulding, overall size 16 x 13 inches (no additional postage and handling required).

---

* IMPORTANT!
These special prices are only available if ordered using the original voucher on this page (no copies permitted) and at the same time as your free Mounted Print, for delivery to the same address

---

Frith Collectors' Guild

From time to time we publish a magazine of news and stories about Frith photographs and further special offers of Frith products. If you would like 12 months FREE membership, please return this form.

Send completed forms to:
The Francis Frith Collection, Frith's Barn, Teffont, Salisbury, Wiltshire SP3 5QP

Voucher for **FREE** and Reduced Price Frith Prints

Picture no.	Page number	Qty	Mounted @ £7.49	Framed + £14.95	Total Cost
		1	**Free of charge***	£	£
			£7.49	£	£
			£7.49	£	£
			£7.49	£	£
			£7.49	£	£
			£7.49	£	£

Please allow 28 days for delivery *** Post & handling**	£2.25
Book Title . . . . **Total Order Cost**	£

Please do not photocopy this voucher. Only the original is valid, so please cut it out and return it to us.

I enclose a cheque / postal order for £ . . . . made payable to 'The Francis Frith Collection'
OR please debit my Mastercard / Visa / Switch / Amex card
(credit cards please on all overseas orders)

Number . . . .

Issue No(Switch only) . . . . .Valid from (Amex/Switch) . . . .

Expires . . . . Signature . . . .

Name Mr/Mrs/Ms . . . .

Address . . . .

. . . .

. . . .

Postcode . . . . Daytime Tel No . . . .

Email Address . . . .

Valid to 31/12/04

The Francis Frith Collectors' Guild
Please enrol me as a member for 12 months free of charge.

Name Mr/Mrs/Ms . . . .

Address . . . .

. . . .

. . . .

. . . . Postcode . . . .

Would you like to find out more about Francis Frith?

We have recently recruited some entertaining speakers who are happy to visit local groups, clubs and societies to give an illustrated talk documenting Frith's travels and photographs. If you are a member of such a group and are interested in hosting a presentation, we would love to hear from you.

Our speakers bring with them a small selection of our local town and county books, together with sample prints. They are happy to take orders. A small proportion of the order value is donated to the group who have hosted the presentation. The talks are therefore an excellent way of fundraising for small groups and societies.

Can you help us with information about any of the Frith photographs in this book?

We are gradually compiling an historical record for each of the photographs in the Frith archive. It is always fascinating to find out the names of the people shown in the pictures, as well as insights into the shops, buildings and other features depicted.

If you recognize anyone in the photographs in this book, or if you have information not already included in the author's caption, do let us know. We would love to hear from you, and will try to publish it in future books or articles.

Our production team

Frith books are produced by a small dedicated team at offices in the converted Grade II listed 18th-century barn at Teffont near Salisbury, illustrated above. Most have worked with the Frith Collection for many years. All have in common one quality: they have a passion for the Frith Collection. The team is constantly expanding, but currently includes:

Jason Buck, John Buck, Douglas Burns, Ruth Butler, Heather Crisp, Isobel Hall, Hazel Heaton, Peter Horne, James Kinnear, Tina Leary, Hannah Marsh, Sue Molloy, Kate Rotondetto, Dean Scource, Eliza Sackett, Terence Sackett, Sandra Sanger, Lewis Taylor, Shelley Tolcher, Clive Wathen and Jenny Wathen.